The Lady
in Kicking Horse
Reservoir

The Lady
in Kicking Horse
Reservoir

by Richard Hugo

Carnegie Mellon University Press
Pittsburgh 1999

Some of these poems appeared in the following publications:

Magazines

Iowa Review	Poetry Northwest	New York
Trace	New American Review	Quarterly
Quarterly Review	Northwest Review	Antaeus
of Literature	The Malahat Review	Madrona
Sage	Sumac	New Letters
Colorado State Review	Field	Seizure
December	Inscape	L'esprit
Carolina Quarterly	Quarry	Gulfstream

"The Only Bar In Dixon" originally appeared in the *New Yorker*. © 1970 The New Yorker Magazine, Inc.

"Point No Point" originally appeared in *Poetry*. © 1966 by the Modern Language Association. Reprinted by permission of the editor of *Poetry*.

Anthologies

"Degrees of Gray in Philipsburg," in addition to appearing in New American Review, appeared in *The Contemporary American Poets*, ed. Mark Strand, The World Publishing Company, Inc., 1969 and in *Reading Modern Poetry*, ed. Paul Engle and Warren Carrier, Scott, Foresman and Company, 1968.

"The Lady in Kicking Horse Reservior," appeared in *The Contemporary American Poets*, ed. Mark Strand, The World Publishing Company, Inc., 1969.

Library of Congress Catalog Card Number 98-74553
ISBN 0-88748-308-9
Copyright © 1973 by Richard Hugo
All rights reserved
Printed and bound in the United States of America

First Carnegie Mellon University Press Edition, March 1999.

The Lady in Kicking Horse Reservoir was first published by W. W. Norton & Company, Inc., New York, in 1973.

The publisher expresses gratitude to James Welch for his assistance in producing this volume.

Publication of this book is supported by gifts to the Classic Contemporaries Series from James W. Hall, Richard M. Cyert (1921-1998), and other anonymous benefactors.

For
  Richard Howard

Many of the poems in this book were written or initiated during 1967–68 when I was in Europe on a Rockefeller Foundation Creative Writing Fellowship. Many thanks to the Foundation for its generosity.

Contents

Montana With Friends

A Map of Montana in Italy

On this map white. A state thick as a fist
or blunt instrument. Long roads weave and cross
red veins full of rage. Big Canada, map maker's
pink, squats on our backs, planning bad winters
for years, and Glacier Park's green with my envy
of Grizzly Bears. On the right, antelope sail
between strands of barbed wire and never
get hurt, west, I think, of Plevna, say near
Sumatra, or more west, say Shawmut,
anyway, on the right, east on the plains.
The two biggest towns are dull deposits
of men getting along, making money, driving
to church every Sunday, censoring movies and books.
The two most interesting towns, Helena, Butte,
have the good sense to fail. There's too much
schoolboy in bars—I'm tougher than you—
and too much talk about money.
Jails and police are how you dream Poland—
odd charges, bad food and forms you must fill
stating your religion. In Poland say none.
With so few Negroes and Jews we've been reduced
to hating each other, dumping our crud
in our rivers, mistreating the Indians.
Each year, 4000 move, most to the west
where ocean currents keep winter in check.
This map is white, meaning winter, ice
where you are, helping children who may be
already frozen. It's white here too
but back of me, up in the mountains where
the most ferocious animals

are obsequious wolves. No one fights
in the bars filled with pastry. There's no
prison for miles. But last night the Italians
cheered the violence in one of our westerns.

for Marjorie Carrier

The Milltown Union Bar
(*Laundromat & Café*)

You could love here, not the lovely goat
in plexiglass nor the elk shot
in the middle of a joke, but honest drunks,
crossed swords above the bar, three men hung
in the bad painting, others riding off
on the phony green horizon. The owner,
fresh from orphan wars, loves too
but bad as you. He keeps improving things
but can't cut the bodies down.

You need never leave. Money or a story
brings you booze. The elk is grinning
and the goat says go so tenderly
you hear him through the glass. If you weep
deer heads weep. Sing and the orphanage
announces plans for your release. A train
goes by and ditches jump. You were nothing
going in and now you kiss your hand.

When mills shut down, when the worst drunk
says finally I'm stone, three men still hang
painted badly from a leafless tree, you
one of them, brains tied behind your back,
swinging for your sin. Or you swing
with goats and elk. Doors of orphanages
finally swing out and here you open in.

for Harold Herndon

5

Where Jennie Used to Swim

The Blackfoot bends, pools deep around
the cliff that bends it, and a brave man arcs down
yelling 'hey.' He splits the river clean. Foam
and his first wave die before they gain
the opposite sand. His cry and his exploded plunge
die in yellow tamarack high above her dream.
When she swam here, boys threw pine cones
at her bobbing hair. Tamarack was green
and promise, both in current and the summer,
hummed as warm as the plane she heard
but couldn't find hummed to glamorous lands.

Promise. Glamor. These thin out after
twenty-five hard winters. Jet engines make
no hum. Not one rattlesnake remains
for boys to nail on a weathered one-by-ten
for a parade through Bonner where
the girls applaud. Heavy August air
compounds the waste, the black smoke pouring
from the mill, the sunning girl reliving
the phone call from the hospital.

The swimmer climbs out chattering. This river
needs no calendar when tamarack turns gold
and someone, loved so much her final day
is rerun like a film each autumn
on the silver pool. The Blackfoot says: you lose
and rivers jump so honestly, even the rejected
cannot call them smug. A woman arcs
and arrows down the rock, her 'hey' gone ringing
up the canyon, her first wave fighting flow.

for Jennie Herndon

6

Where Mission Creek Runs Hard for Joy

Rapids shake the low hung limbs like hair.
In your wine old fields of wheat replay
gold promises of what a kiss would be. In your face
a horse still flogs your face. Whatever is odd,
the Indian without a tribe who dresses mad
in kilts, the cloud that snaps at mountains,
means, to you, life at normal, no rest
from the weird. My obsessions too
ugly out in air and down the driving
water to the dam. We rest easy in these pines.
This run-off, lives or water, leaves us mute.

I fight the sudden cold diminished light
with flashbacks of a blonde, somewhere
outside Bremerton, her face my first sun
and I never knew her name. Was it you
across this table now, all centuries of what
all men find lovely, Mongolian and Serb,
invested in your face still pink from
the winds' slap and that sadistic wheat?
Money's in the creek. Gold stones magnify
to giant coins, and you poise gold alone
on rock above the wealthy water
and the slow swamp of some early bitter scene.

Kiss my wine and pour it down my tongue.
Pour it twisted down my hair. Protective armour
fragments in the creek's roar. You are right
to say the trees here grow too straight.
I am right to bring back all the harsh
bizarre beginning of the dirt, the long beat

of each sun across the cabbage, and the hate
that comes from nowhere, that's accounted for
in photos of ourselves we took and still sneak
looks at late at night. And we are right—
the coins are real, the low hung limbs are hair
and Mission Creek, this wild high run-off
in our mouths is clearly on its way.

for Joy Tweten

Graves at Elkhorn

'Eighty-nine was bad. At least a hundred
children died, the ones with money planted
in this far spot from the town. The corn
etched in these stones was popular that year.
'Our dearest one is gone.' The poorer ones
used wood for markers. Their names
got weaker every winter. Now gray wood
offers a blank sacrifice to rot.

The yard and nearly every grave are fenced.
Something in this space must be defined—
where the lot you paid too much for ends
or where the body must not slide beyond.
The yard should have a limit like the town.
The last one buried here: 1938. The next
to last: 1911 from a long disease.

The fence around the yard is barbed, maintained
by men, around the graves, torn down
by pines. Some have pines for stones.
The yard is this far from the town because
when children die the mother should repeat
some form of labor, and a casual glance
would tell you there could be no silver here.

for Joe Ward

9

St. Ignatius Where the Salish Wail

It's a bad Good Friday, snow and mud
and mongrels in the road. Today's sky said
He'd weigh a ton tonight. A priest
unhooks the hands while Flatheads chant
ninety pounds of spices on the skin.
Another One, not the one they took down from
the cross, is lugged by six old Indians
around the room, five following with songs.

On a real Good Friday, warm and moon,
they'd pack Him outside where bright
fires burn. Here or there, the dialect
burns on their tongues. Elbow joints enflame
and still they crawl
nailed hours to the tomb. For men
who raced young April clouds and won, the pace
of reverence is grim. Their chanting
bangs the door of any man's first cave.

Mongrels have gone home. We slop
toward the car. Every year
a few less live who know the Salish hymns.
The mud is deeper. Snow has turned to rain.
We were renegade when God had gills.
We never change. Still, the raw sound
of their faces and the wailing unpretentious
color of their shawls——

for David and Annick Smith

Bad Eyes Spinning the Rock

Spinning hymns downstream is fun. The worm spins
warm to German Brown, and warm to bad sight
Rock Creek splits the day in hunks a hawk can't count.
A fragment of a trout, half tree, half elk,
dissolves in light and could have been a cliff.
Current and a cross can blind a saint.

A good cast is a loss of mills, of women
knocking five days following the burial,
words that never heal, silk organ droning while
the sermon crawls down empty pews, a plea
for money for electric bells. A cast is cold.
Nylon takes a life to reach the lunker caves.

Booze. The all night all day shack. Sneaking
home to rooms gone gray from piety
and calm. The Rock is ripping walls with horns
and down the cliff, jittering in blur
a hawk or hawks bomb scripture into pine.
A trick of wind: the deep flat run is clear.

All sermons warp with one slight knock.
Eyes are hands. Nylon sings and reassembles day
and day is cracked in silver jokes: whip and tug
and whipping rod, red ladder and white play,
a mottled monster ages down the net,
brighter than answer, big enough to see.

for Warren Carrier

11

Dog Lake With Paula

Snow air in the wind. It stings our lunch sacks,
arcs the nylon line. Being from the farm
you can take forever in your wild face
the boredom of wind across the boring glare.
On the farm, it's wheat. Here, water. Same.
Same blinding. Same remorseless drive
of yesterday and dream. A car starts
on the moon and suffocating caves
the mountain lion leaves are castle halls.

This wind is saying things it said at home.
Paula, go upwind to spawn, years across
the always slanted buffalo grass
and centuries past wheels that mill the water.
Deep in the Bear Tooth range the source of wind
is pulsing like your first man in the wheat.
It's not a source of wisdom. It's a wise mistake.
The wise result: pain of hungry horses,
howl of wild dogs in the blow. You swim upwind
so hard you have become the zany trees.

Look away when the lake glare hurts. Now,
look back. The float is diving. Deep down,
deeper than the lake, a trout is on the line.
We are, we always were, successful dogs.
Prehistoric beaches burn each dawn for loners.
Listen, Paula. Feel. This wind has traveled
all the way around the world, picked up heat
from the Sahara, a new Tasmanian
method of love, howl of the arctic whale.

for Paula Petrik

12

To Die in Milltown

is to have an old but firmly painted name
and friends. The Blackfoot stops, funereal
and green, and eagles headed north
for sanctuary wait for our applause
to fly them home. At 6 A.M.
the fast train east divides the town,
one half, grocery store and mill,
the other, gin and bitter loss.

Even the famed drunk has begun to fail.
His face, fat yesterday and warm, went
slack thin color, one more eerie morning
off the river, bones of ugly women
in his bed. The timber train at noon
divides the town an hour into dying cars.
By four, all bears in the protective hills
hum the air alive. And should the girl
all drunks recall, the full one filled with sun
return, her teeth intact and after 40 years
her charm preserved in joke, the aging drunks
will claim they cheated death with mash.
Death, the Blackfoot says, but never snow.

To die in Milltown, die at 6 P.M.
The fast train west rattles your bourbon warm.
The latest joke is on the early drunk:
sing one more chorus and the nun you love
will dance here out of habit. To live
stay put. The Blackfoot, any river
has a million years to lend, and weather's
always wild to look at down the Hellgate—

solid gray forever trailing off white rain.
Our drinks are full of sun. These aging eagles
climb the river on their own.

for Gene Jarvis

Pishkun

Looking at the model of a pishkun
in the Russell Memorial Museum
you have to think converging walls of rock
back and back ten miles across the plain.
The rest is clear: blind bison driven down
the cliff by Indians disguised as wolves,
and where the bison land, braves
with arrows finishing the twitch.

All for meat and hide. High priest crying
go down buffalo and break. The herd cracking
on the rock below. Scream and dust.
Five hundred tons of violence. Of silence.
A cry to women: bring the cleaning knives.

South of town, in a gulch of lovely
what I guess are aspens, frames of cars
are rusting and discarded shoes discolor
blue with mold. How many hundred tons
of lovers broke that mattress soaking
in the rain a bird shakes off the leaves?
How many, starved on barren claims,
could have used the glitter of those cans?
The world discards the world. Abandoned kilns
stunt the oldest pines. Thick brush
muffles the gurgle of a brook of runoff rain.

Charlie Russell, that fairly good, not really good,
sometimes good with yellow, often good with light,
never good with totals, total man, forgot
the world has garbage. He hangs

in a museum named for him, rare as bison
hung bewildered halfway down the stone.

for Jackie Smith

Reclamation at Coloma

This last estate of greed has been reclaimed
by drone. Slaves crawled down the mountain
to the cities, factories with unions
and a definite rate of pay. Without
indentured help, wells went dry and shafts
were left half dug. Exciting endings
of old True Detectives are obscured by worms
and no two shoes are mates. Only horseflies
prospered and they prosper still.
Bears will always leave tomorrow's meal.
For boredom there are only boring answers.

News thirty years ago remains mold-welded
to the walls. A lady, known to Butte police
as Al, has been arrested with a stolen truck
of beer in Boulder. Something about Hitler
faded where the rain leaked in. Housewives
faded from hard work and harder worry,
the baby sick, the gold slow coming
and the price of gold sung wrong
by men returning early drunk from town.

The drone is firm. Heat, a high prop plane
and insect hum reclaim five frames of cars
stripped clean of everything poverty could use.
Bedsprings are for singles. The broken sluice
could be the work of lightning or a final rage
and what's the difference now? Rats stay on.
The road out is the one the ghost took
years before his body quit and packed—
took off singing morning and did not come back.

for Eric and Kari Johnson

Helena, Where Homes Go Mad

Cries of gold or men about to hang
trail off where the brewery failed
on West Main. Greedy fingernails
ripped the ground up inch by inch
down the gulch until the hope of gold
ran out and men began to pimp.
Gold is where you find it in the groin.

That hill is full of unknown bones.
What was their sin? Rape? A stolen claim?
Not being liked? When the preacher,
sick of fatal groans, cut the gallows down
the vicious rode the long plain north
for antelope, or bit their lips in church.

Years of hawks and nutty architects
and now the lines of some diluted rage
dice the sky for gawkers on the tour.
Also shacks. Also Catholic spires,
the Shriner mosque in answer,
Reeder's Alley selling earthenware.
Nowhere gold. Nowhere men strung up.
Another child delivered, peace,
the roaring bars and what was love
is cut away year after year
or played out vulgar like a game
the bored make up when laws are firm.

Not my country. The sun is too direct,
the air too thin, the dirt road packed
too hard. Someday a man

might walk away alone from violence
and gold, shrinking every step.
A small girl, doomed perhaps
to be a whore might read his early tears.
Let's read the hawks. She'll marry, he
go dry-eyed to the hot plain north
and strong, behind him—Helena
insane with babies and the lines of homes.

for Tom Madden

Silver Star

This is the final resting place of engines,
farm equipment and that rare, never more
than occasional man. Population:
17. Altitude: unknown. For no
good reason you can guess, the woman
in the local store is kind. Old steam trains
have been rusting here so long, you feel
the urge to oil them, to lay new track, to start
the west again. The Jefferson
drifts by in no great hurry on its way
to wed the Madison, to be a tributary
of the ultimately dirty brown Missouri.
This town supports your need to run alone.

What if you'd lived here young, gone full of fear
to that stark brick school, the cruel teacher
supported by your guardian? Think well
of the day you ran away to Whitehall.
Think evil of the cop who found you starving
and returned you, siren open, to the house
you cannot find today. You question
everyone you see. The answer comes back wrong.
There was no house. They never heard your name.

When you leave here, leave in a flashy car
and wave goodbye. You are a stranger
every day. Let the engines and the farm
equipment die, and know that rivers
end and never end, lose and never lose
their famous names. What if your first girl
ended certain she was animal, barking

at the aides and licking floors? You know
you have no answers. The empty school
burns red in heavy snow.

for Bill Kittredge

With Kathy in Wisdom

I only dreamed that high cliff we were on
overlooking Wisdom and the Big Hole drain.
I dreamed us high enough to not see men,
dreamed old land behind us better left
and we were vagabond.

We went twice to Wisdom, not in dream.
Once in day, odd couple after Brooks,
and then at night, dark derelicts
obsessed with fake
false fronts for tourists and the empty church.

I dream the cliff again. Evening. Deep
beneath, Wisdom turning lights on. Neon flakes
are planets when we touch.
I wake up shouting, Wisdom's not that much,
and sweating. Wisdom never will be bright.

Lord, we need sun. We need moon. Fern
and mercy. Form and dream destroyed.
Need the cliff torn down. To hold hands
and stare down the raw void of the day.
Be my contraband.

Three fat Eastern Brook a night, that's
my private limit. The cliff broke
and wind pours in on Wisdom
leaving false fronts really what they seem.
Morning Wisdom, Kathy. It is no dream.

for Kathy McClelland

Indian Graves at Jocko

These dirt mounds make the dead seem fat.
Crude walls of rock that hold the dirt
when rain rides wild, were placed with skill
or luck. No crucifix can make
the drab boards of this chapel Catholic.
A mass across these stones becomes
whatever wail the wind decides is right.

They asked for, got the Black Robe
and the promised masses, well meant
promises, shabby third hand crosses.
This graveyard can expand, can crawl
in all directions to the mountains,
climb the mountains to the salmon
and a sun that toned the arrows
when animals were serious as meat.

The dead are really fat, the houses lean
from lack of loans. The river runs
a thin bed down the useless flat
where Flathead homes are spaced like friends.
The dead are strange
jammed this familial. A cheap fence
separates the chapel from the graves.

A forlorn lot like this, where snow
must crawl to find the tribal stones,
is more than just a grim result of cheat,
Garfield's forgery, some aimless trek
of horses from the stolen Bitter Root.
Dead are buried here because the dead

will always be obscure, wind
the one thing whites will always give a chance.

for Victor Charlo

Touring

Drums in Scotland

Trumpets. A valley opens and beyond
the valley, closed and open sea. This land
is tough north music. Green cannot hide
the rock it hides and if horizon softens
into roll, it is the terrible drums
you dream are rolling. It is a curved sword
carving gray. It is counter roll
to rolling sky. And you were never wanted.

Rain. Small windows muting light until
the living room was dull, a hunger
that would go on hunger for the girl.
No warmth in eyes, arms, anything
but words. No warmth in words. The cat
kept staring and the woman in the kitchen
banged about. What good words were you saying
that the small girl listened? You walked
two miles to visit every Sunday and she
always said come in. No invitation
needed in the country. You just went and lied.

That's a long sky there from Scotland.
Same gray. Same relentless drive
of sky and music. It is your dream,
that terrible rolling drum. You were never
wanted and she always said come in.

Chysauster

Only these stone hut walls record their lives.
We know: not Roman. We speculate them
pastoral and kind. We say the grass is modern
but this gross wind must have been here then
tearing their eyes like ours, blurring the enemy
that never comes. And without trees no love
was secret on this hill. Your hot glance
at a girl exposed you to the grunting god
they hid with cattle in the far hut you were not
allowed to see. Where did they suddenly go,
third century, before Penzance and the discovery
of tin? You have to shout your theory
in this wind and shouted it sounds silly.
Black plague comes back laughter and grass bends
obedient as ancient beets. The size of huts
implies big families or people so communal
they did not use names. No one's found a coin,
something that might indicate exchange.
You loved your sister and she mocked you
as you crawled the dirt toward her, your breathing
muffled by her cackle and the drumming sky.

Walking Praed Street

I've walked this street in far too many towns.
The weather, briefly: in Salerno, rain.
Same scraps of paper blown, same windows
full of girlie mags, the cheap gold lettering
on doors: suits altered. Come in and browse.
What happened to last winter? I am old.
What happened to the boiling oily girl?
The weather, briefly: in Chicago, bum.

I could sound cultured in the drab east end
or sweet in Soho, or in Barclays Limited
(so limited they don't cash Barclays checks)
gracious as I compliment the tube.
I'm learning manners. Thank you very much.
The money stops me. What is 8 and 6?
This is a town of jittering bitter hands.
The weather, briefly: Copenhagen, none.

Tonight I'll hear the jazz in Golders Green.
Tomorrow the Hampstead literary scene.
Next day, up river to the park at Kew
and next day, you. Ah, love, to feed the ravens
in St. James, and that frightfully stuffy,
hopelessly dignified, brazenly British,
somewhat mangy lion in the zoo.
The weather, briefly: in Palermo, snow.

The weather, oddly: in Sofia, luck
brought by an old storm to your window
and rattling off like first remembered hail.
Who's to know you fail and do not fail

and who's to know the banging storm within,
one wind returning empty to your soul
noon after afternoon. Love's possible in Bern.
The weather, always: desolate again.

You live this road forever and no love comes by.
The weather, fondly: in your home town, hurt.
The weather, happily: the same old dirt
you came from: in Seattle, you.
I've walked this street in lots of towns,
always foreign weather at my throat.
Same paper blown, same broken man
begging me for money and I overgive.

Somersby

Mercy Jesus Mercy
cries a stone
b 1586
d 1591
and Tennyson's brook
drones on

The Prado: Bosch: S. Antonio

Most men are rodents clothed. After fun
they mount pale fish and ride away, or lead cows
home to farms where every noon a wife explodes.
Saints do not erupt or disappear in vapor-trails
of life well burned. Saints sit bored alone
and play the old flood out again, complete,
completely sad, the river's flimsy green
buckling the home that might have stood a lifetime,
anchored by the woman's hostile face.
The daughter in the doorway, nude, expected nothing.
Crying love me to the swimmer was a gesture.

That huge face warped by failure, sun men or soil,
weighs on the saint, supports a second home
the river also ruins. Huge, yes and heaven
is white air. Hell is where you are, a table
bare but for the apple you don't want to eat.
A saint finds hunger holier than prayer
and life must be repeated empty, played back
every day, no variation. Sister must stay bitter
seated in high water, playing solitaire.
And rats must ride the winged translucent carp
into the ether, using their tails to whip
that little extra speed from fins before
oblivion's insured. The saint will live forever
replaying that watery hate day after day,
getting bigger until the picture
is a portrait. Even now his face outgrows
the woman, the explosion and the river.

The Prado: Number 2671, *Anonimo Español*

A little guts, self drama and it's done.
I understand you, two six seven one,
leaving the white fat town behind like that
safe in the moat, at every gate two cops
with spears insisting lovers on the drawbridge
chat within the rules. All bridges lead
to paths that lead to churches. The sea
and ship are so remote, to notice them
you violate the charm. Towers sparkle,
banners flutter clean. But in your last few dreams
rats nibbled at your arms. The king proclaimed
no peeking at the royal pornography bank.

The upper picture, granted not well painted,
hurt them. You, vertical spread eagle,
no perspective with your floggers
who admitted you were nice. You said
when men are dead, stars can talk to rivers,
glad clouds need never part. They said
what art. I say rivers run from towns
and torture out of paintings, why not man?

I'm plenty less than you. Call me forty-four.
Old enough to know what happened at the door.
They kept your things, said get out, die in weather.
Dogs will eat you where the only love's exposure
and there's dead rain between mother and your mouth.
We like it here. The drawbridge thundered down.
A cop said so long, friend—he wasn't one—

and you died quietly away behind a smile
you knew they'd find among your birds
and dogs, one dog crosseyed, ineffectual,
old, the other ferocious, black,
his teeth, the peacock and your hand
guarding your groin from the rook.

At Cronkhite

Light bangs empty barracks where
a corporal waits for orders
from the sea. The highest tide
since Caesar swept all wood away.
New huts are planned in China
and the urge to enmity
dries in wind that rips a banner into rag,
the wrong word from my mouth. Raw day
and cormorants are blazing over sand.

This debris is pure. The next girl
will come burning from the foam,
my name her checkpoint and my tongue
her navigational fix. It's official now:
the Army will return. This beach will roar
with cannon. Cormorants will dive
where sun began reflecting and the bones
of lovers shift with no help from the moon.

Kiss me wind and city white. The gate
is never golden and the green teeth
of a jumper rattle off the rock
each violent wave. My orders are:
find wood but don't invoke the tide.
I trust the hum, the next wave starting
from a continent of girls. I trust
I'll die but never Christmas day.

They'll say, he's gone. And someone:
good for him. The raw blaze of the void
might bring me wood tomorrow,

a hundred girls on whales all crying help.
I smile at China and memories of docks.
A dock here would be fatal. No rock wall
protecting piles from thrust and glare.
And what boat would stop here, sea whipped ladies
on the deck throwing me their eyes?

Upper Voight's, To All the Cutthroat There

You curve in dandelion wine and in
my dream of a receptive east. Windows
in my house are sanctuary and the four
hills east are fast with creeks
you live in. Why curve tornado from
the shade of cress or stone, why curve away
when I approach upwind, a bush toward
your home, that home of words in back
of any rock that pools the water dark?

I sneak fat and weightless on the log
you're under. I taste the chinese red
of thunder on your throat, jet spots
on your side that fade to spotless white
along your gut. What prayer brings you roaring
quick as words, unexpected, cruel
through gold? God is small. The wing
of eastbound liners six miles over us
is rigid as your fin when you don't move.

Such climb down. Logs left by the blaze
are hollow and I'm cut from crashing
through black crust. Vine maple, greasewood
and my past including last night
work against my search. And still I look,
certain you'll leave me, a bitter nun
starved for curve in my poem.

Taneum Creek

I don't come here after June when rattlesnakes
come out of caves and snore on stones
along the stream, though trout and trout remain
and I am keen to harm. Yellow bells have fangs
and jack pines rattle in the slightest wind.

The Gold Man on the Beckler

Let him pan. His sluice will rot and flake.
Here, the gold is river, coiling gold
around gold stones or bouncing gold down
flat runs where the riffles split the light.
With just that shack he built beside the stream
how could he get so fat? Where's the food from?
Why so cheerful with a flimsy roof,
no money and that crude hair in his ears?

What put him this far from the world?
Be out of your way in a minute. No cat
dies at home. Even as your spit lands
on my neck, I swear to you my bones
will not impose. Let the world have lovers.
Alders hide me and the crashing river
muffles any cry my other mouth might make.

If I could live like him, my skin stained gold
from this gold stream, I'd change my name.
I have to find a trout or something bright
but hidden by refraction, heavier than sin.
That's why today, my last day here,
while he is rinsing blankets in the river,
before I go that long east to my gold
I shout my best goodbye across the roar.

Touring With Friends

Cataldo Mission

We come here tourist on a bad sky day,
warm milk at 15,000 and the swamp across
the freeway blinding white. No theory
to explain the lack of saint, torn tapestry.
Pews seem built for pygmies, and a drunk
once damned mosquitoes from the pulpit,
raging red with Bible and imagined plague.
Their spirits buoyed, pioneers left running
for the nothing certain nowhere west.
Somewhere, say where Ritzville is, they would
remember these crass pillars lovely
and a moving sermon they had never heard.

More's bad here than just the sky. The valley
we came in on: Mullan. Wallace. Jokes
about the whores. Kellogg and, without salvation,
Smelterville. A stream so slate with crap
the name pollutes the world. Man will die again
to do this to his soul. And over the next hill
he never crosses, promises: love, grass,
a white cathedral, glandular revival
and a new trout, three tall dorsal fins.

We exit from the mission, blind. The haze
still hangs amplifying glare until
two centuries of immigrants in tears
seem natural as rain. The hex is on.
The freeway covers arrows, and the swamp
a spear with feathers meaning stop.
This dry pale day, cars below crawl thirsty,
500 miles to go before the nation quits.

for Jim and Lois Welch

43

Montgomery Hollow

Birds here should have names so hard to say
you name them over. They finally found
the farmer hanging near the stream.
Only insect hum today and the purple odor
of thyme. You'd bet your throat against
the way a mind goes bad. You conquer loss
by going to the place it happened
and replaying it, saying the name
of the face in the open casket right.

People die in cities. Unless it's war
you never see the bodies. They die in print,
over phones in paramouric flats.
Here, you find them staring down the sun,
flies crawling them like bacon. Wives
scream two days running and the pain is gone.
Here, you find them living.

To know a road you own it, every bend
and pebble and the weeds along it,
dust that itches when the August hayrake
rambles home. You own the home.
You own the death of every bird you name.
To live good, keep your life and the scene.
Cow, brook, hay: these are names of coins.

for Stanley Kauffmann

The End of Krim's Pad

When they plan a freeway thru a city
they plan it deliberately thru places
you love most. They take out houses people
lived in years and people die in face
of the fear of loss. We call this progress.
We sweep their elderly bones out of sight
under the concrete carpet. If you have nothing
but a place to hide in, cage cave or kingdom,
a desperate paradise for the infirm, you lose.
You are the one the wreckers look for.

Fifteen years of Herman's various herds,
Cutty Sark and black whores curling on your floor
will not impress them. They will crowd around
and wonder why you're crying when the steel ball swings.
Some will offer advice: stay calm, attend
the church of your choice. You cannot tell them
wounded animals return to die in places
they found food when young. Good things happened here.
One black whore never ages in your dreams.

The building crashes. Plaster. Glass. The twisted
ends of toilet pipe. The repetitious phrases
of embarrassment: I'm sane now, sane and home.
No room you find to live in will be home. You drag
along the brute streets of this world, hunting
what we hunt, hurting when we can't. Stay homeless,
doomed to hound those human meanings we forget
every morning when gray light that might be
any time of day fights like a wounded dog

thru odors of used air, the whore beside you
purring in her dark expensive sleep.

for Seymour Krim

Old Map of Uhlerstown

This map defines your home. The names
are coy bones now. The spillway's worn,
the floodgate stuck half-closed from age.
Under leaves that pile before the dam,
goldfish nose the surface for a meal.
This canal knows all, how style
must find a corner in the world
or die. You built that strong rock wall.

You commit forever to this charm—
bad luck in France—no money—fights.
If everyone you helped came here
you'd need a bigger map. From hills
behind you hawks fall suddenly as hate
to join you on the porch and chat
of cardinals and frozen waterwheels.

Lovers loved beneath that sycamore.
See them on the map, two dots on the lawn,
clawing as the sad canal goes by.
Wind is never cartographic line.
Real leaves fall. First blood of love is dry.
When wet it mapped a home that waited
sheltering the dead until you came.

for Jackson and Marthiel Mathews

A Night With Cindy at Heitman's

Outside: forecasts of humiliating storms.
We're both warm from Jim Beam and bad jokes
understood. One thing about hard wind—
no one fights in it. Loud air takes the place
of rage. You climbed a trembling chair
to see if you were lovely in the mirror.
Daddy's face was stuck there, blank and waiting
to be claimed. If you scream now as then
it will go unnoticed as the oaks crack off.

Storms are memories of old storms at the door.
Don't let them in. Just name them. I say shame,
the poverty, mundane and in the mind.
Hundreds of others with money next door happy.
You do not belong. When bells rang
your invitation to the wedding wild across
the lake, you had a boat and shabby clothes.

Hours of pool balls click. The liquor clicks.
The jukebox booms out fun I thought was dead.
My head is rolling full of ocean. You
are swimming countercurrent, your fin
resilient. You should have a weather
all your own. I've fantasized a thousand homes
to live in. You're in all of them and not in one.
Sweet derelict, your eyes spit
man's first bad weather back at it.

for Cynthia Keyworth

Point No Point

Even in July, from this point north
the sea is rough. Today the wind is treason
tearing at our flag and kicking that commercial
trawl around. We and salmon are beached
or driven down. A need to respond
to defeat—the need to go far—
A Cadillac blooming with girls—
is heritage the gulls who peel off now
across the strait to Double Bluff find fun.

Those cream cliffs miles across the sea
are latent friends. Seabirds are remote
enough to go unnamed, unnamed enough
to laugh a favorite harm away. Waves
go on buffooning and cheap stitching gives
and one bird is Old Betsy flapping north.

I know a flat and friendless north.
A poem can end there, or a man, but never
in a storm. The southbound tanker
cruises by unbudged by slamming waves.
Great bulk often wins and you and I
are fat and sipping beer and waiting
for this storm to rearrange the light,
for birds to come back named, with jokes
and for the sea to weaken, just enough
to kick back home on, never weak
as cream or flat as a summer lake.

for John Duffy Mitchell

Cornwall, Touring

We found the sea in pieces at Pendeen.
Sky was gray above our fun and loud
and rock split perfectly from rock to prove
the Continental Drift. Brazil fits tight
in Africa. We spoke one tongue before
we couldn't hear each other in that weather.
We found the sea in patches red from tin.

We found it white with fear along
the edges, black out deep with shags
racked croaking last year in the oil.
We saw bubble trails of nervous fish
twist through slabs of green, the alternating
gull and ghost of gull in sky
carved hot by lightning.

The dying young die slowly like a lawn.
That grass died wild, a suicidal dive
to pieces of Brazil. Water pounded rock
with favored odds and open tin shafts
played odd tunes we used to hear
at home when we were dying,
odds against the travel in our blood.

Farmers slide into wives the way
waves enter coves and bring us spectrums.
Our lives glint at us off those broken
bits of glass, stained windows
we broke out through, bottles of cheap wine.
We found the sea in pieces at Pendeen,
rock breaking off and rock homes far apart.

for Marion Codd

Shark Island

Sun in our sails, our hooker wheels again
and again through the pollack school.
Our radio sends music through the village
you find sad, nine gray homes deserted
and no P.O. We toast our heavy catch
with stout. We lean back under a sky
wide as spread arms, sparkling with scales.
We are transported by our captain's hand
and breeze, are free and feel it under
those tortured rocks that tower and plunge
deep in green compounded by depth.
We are sailing an ocean and young.

The village nags. It dips and climbs, curves
by every pass we make through pollack
and it dies each time we see it. Where
are they? Were they happy? Did it hurt
to leave? We might grow old here, feed on
light from water and simple events—
the weekly boat with food from Bofin,
waving at hookers, pointing mute directions
on a noisy day. We might fake wisdom:
we have lived here long and understand
the urge to nothing, to a life inside.

Isn't it better, this wheeling, this sun
in our sails and the radio playing,
again and again through the school
with our greed. Monks get odd,
and without fans, hermits rage in caves.
Better to head for a loud port
where homes are loaded and the mail arrives.

for Ann Jeffrey

51

The Tinker Camp

Whatever they promise for money, luck,
a lifetime of love, they promise empty.
They beg us cruel ways, forlorn hand
stuck at us, pathetic face, or watch us
with dead eyes through rags they hung to dry.
They have cheated the last two centuries,
have lied and are hated, have stolen from
the unorganized poor. Even pans they sell
seem made of mean tin, and their wagons
gypsy as kisses you imagine when young.
Always the necessary, dreaded 'move on'.
They never park where we might picnic,
but camp on bare ground, just off roads
where dust from traffic cakes food,
police can eye and insult them, and access
to that long road out of scorn is near.
Our accent and our rental car are signals:
Steal. Beg. Don't feel anything. Don't dream.
They sleep well with our money. We
are the world that will not let them weep.

for Susan Lydiatt

Cleggan

The mackerel are in. Came on the in tide
inside the quay. Word went from boy to boy
and now they're trapped, a net between them
and the open sea, the out tide on the way.
A day of gift. The early out tide
left two sting ray on the flat. Two years ago today
lightning ruined the Martello tower.
The English ghost ran from Ireland free.

Boys throw rocks at mackerel and mackerel
go frantic up and down the draining trap.
Years of thick hands beating grief against
wild air that roared the hooker fleet to hell
and now a meal comes easy. We can wait,
drink stout and sing, certain
prayers unanswered all those years were heard.

Ireland is free. The young leave every year
for England and the bad jobs there. Pretty girls
stay virgin and the old men brag of nothing.
It's something to go on when life's as empty
as the sea of anything but life, swimming
way down aimless, most of it uncaught.
The mackerel are out. Went on the out tide
through a faint gap between net and quay.
It's an Irish day. A tinker boy, eyes far
on the Atlantic, asks why water angers
without warning and takes back unwanted meat.

for Richard Murphy

Crinan Canal

There was never danger in this black sad water.
Not one monster. Not one cruel event along
the bank. It was peaceful even when that carnage
raged up north. The plague passed by
without one victim, and if a barge
hauled contraband, the tedious rhythm
of its cruise always made the mean cop sleep.
The captain of the tug arrived from upstream country
angry: they still sing about the girl
who threw the lock gate open at the curve.

The danger is the world reflected off the black.
The peace of maple shade is doubled. Silence
is compounded until wrens are roaring
and the soft plunk of a frog goes off
beside us bang. Fields that never meant
a lover harm slant eerie, and the next town
promises no language or a stove.

We have followed and followed it down,
past farm and kiln, the seldom used repair shop,
the warm creak of rusted lock gate gears,
unattended locks and wild vines thick
as the quiet, and here's the end: the town
and stores sell candy. The final gate swings open.
The black canal turns generous and green
and issues gifts, barges, tugs and sailboats
to the open world. Never was a danger
and they float out, foam out, sail out, loud.

for Arnold and Adele Tamarin

54

Montana

The Lady in Kicking Horse Reservoir

Not my hands but green across you now.
Green tons hold you down, and ten bass curve
teasing in your hair. Summer slime
will pile deep on your breast. Four months of ice
will keep you firm. I hope each spring
to find you tangled in those pads
pulled not quite loose by the spillway pour,
stars in dead reflection off your teeth.

Lie there lily still. The spillway's closed.
Two feet down most lakes are common gray.
This lake is dark from the black blue Mission range
climbing sky like music dying Indians once wailed.
On ocean beaches, mystery fish
are offered to the moon. Your jaws go blue.
Your hands start waving every wind.
Wave to the ocean where we crushed a mile of foam.

We still love there in thundering foam
and love. Whales fall in love with gulls
and tide reclaims the Dolly skeletons
gone with a blast of aching horns to China.
Landlocked in Montana here
the end is limited by light, the final note
will trail off at the farthest point we see,
already faded, lover, where you bloat.

All girls should be nicer. Arrows rain
above us in the Indian wind. My future
should be full of windy gems, my past

will stop this roaring in my dreams.
Sorry. Sorry. Sorry. But the arrows sing:
no way to float her up. The dead sink
from dead weight. The Mission range
turns this water black late afternoons.

One boy slapped the other. Hard.
The slapped boy talked until his dignity
dissolved, screamed a single 'stop'
and went down sobbing in the company pond.
I swam for him all night. My only suit
got wet and factory hands went home.
No one cared the coward disappeared.
Morning then: cold music I had never heard.

Loners like work best on second shift.
No one liked our product and the factory closed.
Off south, the bison multiply so fast
a slaughter's mandatory every spring
and every spring the creeks get fat
and Kicking Horse fills up. My hope is vague.
The far blur of your bones in May
may be nourished by the snow.

The spillway's open and you spill out
into weather, lover down the bright canal
and mother, irrigating crops
dead Indians forgot to plant.
I'm sailing west with arrows to dissolving foam
where waves strand naked Dollys.
Their eyes are white as oriental mountains
and their tongues are teasing oil from whales.

Ovando

Dust that clouded your last drunk dream
thickens in this degrading wind.
Sage uproots and rolls and ducks streak over
every day, reconnaissance, one inch
out of range. If you need meat, resort
to money, never charm. The weak ghost
of a horse demands false fronts, lean poles
to tie your wife to, automatic love
you and the town hate to make to clouds.

Not all dreams slide away. Not every river
travels south whatever maps might claim.
If you were mapped the color would be wrong,
no brown adequate for harm, no white
white enough for pain. The mountain
wise from battering ages of this wind
fakes a place among the hills. The wise bird
leaves each downwind chance for black holes
high in ice. You can plant yourself forever
and still wobble every storm.

Your life is sediment in your glass,
broken girls you never broke until
the world reissued storms. This is where you stop.
Even here, the women smell you out.
Wind this wild has always brought them freaks.
One smile a week will do. If dry air turns
what had been anger brittle, you
can fragment at pale leisure, one hair
at a time, one nose, one arm, all flaking

slowly until all of you is gone
except some silhouette, obese, passed out in dust.
Old women may have noticed but they say hello.

Driving Montana

The day is a woman who loves you. Open.
Deer drink close to the road and magpies
spray from your car. Miles from any town
your radio comes in strong, unlikely
Mozart from Belgrade, rock and roll
from Butte. Whatever the next number,
you want to hear it. Never has your Buick
found this forward a gear. Even
the tuna salad in Reedpoint is good.

Towns arrive ahead of imagined schedule.
Absorakee at one. Or arrive so late—
Silesia at nine—you recreate the day.
Where did you stop along the road
and have fun? Was there a runaway horse?
Did you park at that house, the one
alone in a void of grain, white with green
trim and red fence, where you know you lived
once? You remembered the ringing creek,
the soft brown forms of far off bison.
You must have stayed hours, then drove on.
In the motel you know you'd never seen it before.

Tomorrow will open again, the sky wide
as the mouth of a wild girl, friable
clouds you lose yourself to. You are lost
in miles of land without people, without
one fear of being found, in the dash
of rabbits, soar of antelope, swirl
merge and clatter of streams.

Montana Ranch Abandoned

Cracks in eight log buildings, counting sheds
and outhouse, widen and a ghost peeks out.
Nothing, tree or mountain, weakens wind
coming for the throat. Even wind must work
when land gets old. The rotting wagon tongue
makes fun of girls who begged to go to town.
Broken brakerods dangle in the dirt.

Alternatives were madness or a calloused moon.
Wood they carved the plowblade from
turned stone as nameless gray. Indifferent flies
left dung intact. One boy had to leave
when horses pounded night, and miles away
a neighbor's daughter puked. Mother's cry
to dinner changed to caw in later years.

Maybe raiding bears or eelworms made them quit,
or daddy died, or when they planted wheat
dead Flatheads killed the plant. That stove
without a grate can't warm the ghost.
Tools would still be good if cleaned, but mortar
flakes and log walls sag. Even if you shored,
cars would still boom by beyond the fence, no glance
from drivers as you till the lunar dust.

2433 Agnes, First Home, Last House in Missoula

It promises quiet here. A green Plymouth
has been a long time sitting across the street.
The lady in 2428 limps with a cane
and west of me fields open all the way
to the mountains, all the way I imagine
to the open sea. A three colored dog
doesn't bark, and between 2428
and 24 I see blocks away a chicken coop
in disrepair, what in the distance seems
moss on the roof and for certain
the windows out, for terribly certain
no chickens, and for beautifully sure
a gray pile of lumber in a vacant lot.

My first morning is cloudy. A rumpled
dirty sheet of clouds is crawling northeast,
not threatening rain, but obscuring
the Rattlesnake range. In 2430
a woman is moving, muted to ghost behind
dotted swiss curtains. She drives
a pale green Falcon. This neighborhood
seems a place where lives, like cars, go on
a long time. It has few children.

I'm somewhat torn. On one hand, I believe
no one should own land. You can't respect
what you own. Better we think of spirits
as owning the land, and use it wisely, giving
back at least as much as we take, repaying

land with Indian rituals of thanks.
And I think when we buy, just the crude fact
of money alone means we really pay out
some part of self we should have retained.
On the other hand, at least fifty buntings
are nervously pecking my lawn.

Ghosts at Garnet

Shacks are brown, big where things were sold,
wheat or girls, small where miners lived.
Some fell while we were crawling up the hill.
Standing shacks are pale. Old weeds believe
in Spring. The man with gun is good
on what the Chinese did. He'll go down
finding veins. A man who missed the vein
two feet was found by golden friends.

Pines are staking claims. Hard rock men
went harder hearing Chinese sticks explode.
The suicide, two feet from girls, believed
east eyes can see through rock. A hawk
was oriental, swinging far too silent
when the mail arrived. Five bars are gone
and recreation, violent and hot.

War drove them out. The latest envelope
is postmarked 'forty-two, the letter shot.
A pine impales the ore cart as if horses
left the cart, a target for the gunning sprouts.
What endures is what we have neglected:
tins that fed them, rusting now in piles.
For weeds all Mays are equal yellow.
Beneath our skin, gold veins
run wild to China. That false front on
the bar that stands is giving. Ghosts are drinking,
reading postcards, claiming stakes in men.

A Night at the Napi in Browning

These Indians explain away their hair
between despair and beer. Two pass out
unnoticed on the floor. One answers to a cop
for children left five hours in a car.
Whatever I came here for, engagement
with the real, tomorrow's trip to Babb,
the first words spoken 'white man'
split my tongue. I buy a round of beer
no phonier than my money is wrong.

Whatever story, I hear between the lines
the novel no one wants. A small aunt
whipped the brave who grovels now
in puke and odd hymns at my feet.
A squaw says no help from the mountains.
The Blood who stole her husband
breaks up all day in her beer. Children
drink us in through windows ten years thick.

It never ends, this brutal way we crack
our lives across our backs. With luck
we'll be soft derelicts. The next sun
is no softer, and I guess what good moons
must have said to them, some round white
ringing lie about the future—trout and kiss,
no ownership of sky and herds returning
fat from ritual songs. The moon outside
lights the alley to familiar hells.

And I, a Mercury outside, a credit card,
a job, a faded face—what should I do?
Go off shaggy to the mountains,
a spot remote enough to stay unloved
and die in flowers, stinking like a bear?

Camas Prairie School

The schoolbell rings and dies before
the first clang can reach the nearest farm.
With land this open, wind is blowing
when there is no wind. The gym's so ugly
victory leaves you empty as defeat,
and following whatever game
you will remember lost, you run fast
slow miles home through grain,
knowing you'll arrive too late
to eat or find the lights on.

Flat and vast. Each farm beyond
a gunshot of the next. A friend
is one you love to walk to, 28 below.
A full moon makes this prairie moon
and horses in a thick night
sound like bears. When your sister's raped
help is out of range. Father's far
from Mother and a far bell's
always ringing you can't hear.

The teacher either must be new each year
or renewed forever. Old photos
show her just as gray beside the class
of '35. Indians rehearse
the Flag Salute, and tourists
on their way to Hot Springs wave.
The road beside the school goes either way.
The last bell rings. You run again,
the only man going your direction.

Missoula Softball Tournament

This summer, most friends out of town
and no wind playing flash and dazzle
in the cottonwoods, music of the Clark Fork stale,
I've gone back to the old ways of defeat,
the softball field, familiar dust and thud,
pitcher winging drops and rises, and wives,
the beautiful wives in the stands, basic, used,
screeching runners home, infants unattended
in the dirt. A long triple sails into right center.
Two men on. Shouts from dugout: go, Ron, go.
Life is better run from. Distance to the fence,
both foul lines and dead center, is displayed.

I try to steal the tricky manager's signs.
Is hit-and-run the pulling of the ear?
The ump gives pitchers too much low inside.
Injustice? Fraud? Ancient problems focus
in the heat. Bad hop on routine grounder.
Close play missed by the team you want to win.
Players from the first game, high on beer,
ride players in the field. Their laughter
falls short of the wall. Under lights, the moths
are momentary stars, and wives, the beautiful wives
in the stands now take the interest they once feigned,
oh, long ago, their marriage just begun, years
of helping husbands feel important just begun,
the scrimping, the anger brought home evenings
from degrading jobs. This poem goes out to them.
Is steal-of-home the touching of the heart?

Last pitch. A soft fly. A can of corn
the players say. Routine, like mornings,
like the week. They shake hands on the mound.
Nice grab on that shot to left. Good game. Good game.
Dust rotates in their headlight beams.
The wives, the beautiful wives are with their men.

Phoning from Sweathouse Creek

I got three bulls and a native cutthroat, lover.
I'm phoning from the bar in Victor.
One drunk's fading fast. The other's fast
with information—worms don't work in August.
I found a virgin forest with a moss floor.
You and I can love there. Pack the food.
Sweathouse tumbles and where the bank
and cedar roots say this is where the shy cut
is, he is, and he comes lightning
out of nothing at your egg. Best of all,
the color. It could be the water, but the bulls
are damn near gold and their white dots
stark as tile. The orange spots flare
like far off fires. The body's tubular and hard.
Cuts are rose and peach, all markings definite
as evil, with a purple gill. The drunk
passed out just now. It's like a ritual.
They put him on a table where he snores.
They named it Sweathouse Creek because
somewhere way upstream from here
the Indians built houses over hot springs
where the sick could sweat bad spirits out.
That's the jukebox. The other drunk can't hear.
Screw him. This is August. I used worms.
But lover, the color, the markings on
the bulls and cuts, and that deep forest
and the moss—

The Only Bar in Dixon

Home. Home. I knew it entering.
Green cheap plaster and the stores
across the street toward the river
failed. One Indian depressed
on Thunderbird. Another buying
Thunderbird to go. This air
is fat with gangsters I imagine
on the run. If they ran here
they would be running from
imaginary cars. No one cares
about the wanted posters
in the brand new concrete block P.O.

This is home because some people
go to Perma and come back
from Perma saying Perma
is no fun. To revive, you take 382
to Hot Springs, your life savings
ready for a choice of bars, your hotel
glamorous with neon up the hill.
Is home because the Jocko
dies into the Flathead. Home because
the Flathead goes home north northwest.

I want home full of grim permission.
You can go as out of business here
as rivers or the railroad station.
I knew it entering.
                    Five bourbons
and I'm in some other home.

Dixon

Light crawls timid over fields
from some vague source behind the hills,
too gray to be the sun. Any morning
brings the same, a test of stamina,
your capacity to live the long day out
paced by the hesitant river. No chance
you might discover someone dead.
Always you curse the limited goods
in the store and your limited money.
You learn to ignore the wind leak
in your shack. On bad days in the bar
you drink until you are mayor.

On neutral days you hope the school
is adequate though you're no father
and your wife left decades back
when the train still ran. You look
hours down the track. Perhaps a freight.
Only the arrogant wind. You think
the browns are running, hitting bait.
You have waited and waited for mail,
a wedding invitation, a postcard
from New York. You reread the book
about red lovers one more time,
pages torn and the cover gone.

On good days festive cars streak by.
You laugh and wave. Sun on blacktop
whirrs like ancient arrows in the sky.
Cattails flash alive the way they did
when lightning told them, die.

You catch the river in its flowing
never flowing frozen glide.
The small clear river jitters on
to join the giant green one lumbering
a definite west, a lake released.
Your heroes go home green. Bison
on the range are reproducing bears.

Hot Springs

You arrived arthritic for the cure,
therapeutic qualities of water
and the therapeutic air. Twenty-five
years later you limp out of bars
hoping rumors will revive, some doctor
will discover something curative
in natural steam. You have a choice
of abandoned homes to sleep in.
Motels constructed on the come
went broke before the final board
was nailed. Operative still:
your tainted fantasy and the delux hotel.

You have ached taking your aches up the hill.
Another battery of tests. Terrible probe
of word and needle. Always the fatal word—
when we get old we crumble. They wave
from the ward and you creak back down
to streets with wide lots between homes.
When that rare tourist comes, you tell him
you're not forlorn. There are advantages here—
easy pace of day, slow circle of sun.

If some day a cure's announced, for instance
the hot springs work, you will walk young
again in Spokane, find startling women,
you wonder why you feel empty and frown
and why goodbyes are hard. You go out healthy
on the gray thin road and when you look back
no one is waving. They kept no record
of your suffering, wouldn't know you
if you returned, without your cane, your grin.

Bear Paw

The wind is 95. It still pours from the east
like armies and it drains each day of hope.
From any point on the surrounding rim,
below, the teepees burn. The wind
is infantile and cruel. It cries 'give in' 'give in'
and Looking Glass is dying on the hill.
Pale grass shudders. Cattails beg and bow.
Down the draw, the dust of anxious horses
hides the horses. When it clears, a car
with Indiana plates is speeding to Chinook.

That bewildering autumn, the air howled
garbled information and the howl of coyotes
blurred the border. Then a lull in wind.
V after V of Canada geese. Silence
on the highline. Only the eternal nothing
of space. This is Canada and we are safe.
You can study the plaques, the unique names
of Indians and bland ones of the whites,
or study books, or recreate from any point
on the rim the action. Marked stakes tell you
where they fell. Learn what you can. The wind
takes all you learn away to reservation graves.

If close enough to struggle, to take blood
on your hands, you turn your weeping face
into the senile wind. Looking Glass is dead
and will not die. The hawk that circles overhead
is starved for carrion. One more historian
is on the way, his cloud on the horizon.

Five years from now the wind will be 100,
full of Joseph's words and dusting plaques.
Pray hard to weather, that lone surviving god,
that in some sudden wisdom we surrender.

Degrees of Gray in Philipsburg

You might come here Sunday on a whim.
Say your life broke down. The last good kiss
you had was years ago. You walk these streets
laid out by the insane, past hotels
that didn't last, bars that did, the tortured try
of local drivers to accelerate their lives.
Only churches are kept up. The jail
turned 70 this year. The only prisoner
is always in, not knowing what he's done.

The principal supporting business now
is rage. Hatred of the various grays
the mountain sends, hatred of the mill,
The Silver Bill repeal, the best liked girls
who leave each year for Butte. One good
restaurant and bars can't wipe the boredom out.
The 1907 boom, eight going silver mines,
a dance floor built on springs—
all memory resolves itself in gaze,
in panoramic green you know the cattle eat
or two stacks high above the town,
two dead kilns, the huge mill in collapse
for fifty years that won't fall finally down.

Isn't this your life? That ancient kiss
still burning out your eyes? Isn't this defeat
so accurate, the church bell simply seems
a pure announcement: ring and no one comes?
Don't empty houses ring? Are magnesium
and scorn sufficient to support a town,
not just Philipsburg, but towns

of towering blondes, good jazz and booze
the world will never let you have
until the town you came from dies inside?

Say no to yourself. The old man, twenty
when the jail was built, still laughs
although his lips collapse. Someday soon,
he says, I'll go to sleep and not wake up.
You tell him no. You're talking to yourself.
The car that brought you here still runs.
The money you buy lunch with,
no matter where it's mined, is silver
and the girl who serves you food
is slender and her red hair lights the wall.